# ENGLISH QUILTING

## OLD & NEW

1. Devon Quilt in White Linen, circa. 1840. Note Floral Centre encircled by "Fern."
Hearts in Corners symbolising a Marriage Quilt.

# ENGLISH QUILTING
## OLD & NEW

WITH NOTES ON ITS WEST COUNTRY TRADITION

*By*

ELIZABETH HAKE

*Illustrated from Photographs & Diagrams*

B. T. BATSFORD LTD, LONDON

ISBN 0 7134 5872 0

Printed and bound in Great Britain by
Butler & Tanner Ltd, Frome and London
for the publishers
B. T. Batsford Ltd
4 Fitzhardinge Street
London W1H 0AH

Cover shows a West Country quilt of 1825 (*private collection*).

# PREFACE

THIS book does not pretend to be an exhaustive treatise on a subject which must continue to lead to new discoveries as each scrap of its interesting history comes to light, but it does claim to be of possible service to those needlewomen, who without it might miss the opportunity and pleasure of experimenting in an almost forgotten industry, full of regional character and folk-lore.

It is common knowledge that English quilting, not merely as a craft or pastime, but as a home-industry, has steadily persisted in the northern counties of Durham and Northumberland, and in Wales. So much has this industry been supported and encouraged during the past few years that the attention and admiration of other parts of England have developed into a desire to emulate. Unfortunately no attempt appears so far to have been made by enthusiasts to trace examples of the work of their own local ancestresses. The tendency has been to learn "foreign" designs and technique from the districts where quilting still survives; thus quilters from Durham and Wales have become teachers in Devon and Somerset.

Through a fortunate chance an authentic Devon quilt (Frontispiece, 11) nearly one hundred years old, was discovered in 1933, and the peculiar details of its design led to research which resulted in the contents of this volume, and to the conclusion that quilting as a home-industry may have been universal in England up to fifty years ago. If a survey of each county could be made within the next few years, it is reasonably certain that some remarkable evidence in support of this theory would be forthcoming from the last remaining traces of this fascinating art.

In the West of England it is still just possible to establish *direct* contact in a few rare instances, with women who have actually themselves been quilters within the last sixty years. Three of these veterans have most cordially entered into the spirit of the local search, helping as far as possible to recall examples of design and practice, which they personally learned from their mothers and grandmothers, and personally carried out. To have been taught by them is to have acquired firsthand knowledge wherewith to keep the art of quilting alive, in this way qualifying by direct continuity for passing it on to others.

It should be explained that care has been taken to establish the regional origin of the quilts illustrated in this book, by ascertaining the parentage of their makers.

To Mrs. FitzRandolph, of the Rural Industries Bureau, much gratitude is due for her help and co-operation throughout the past two years. Her experience of Welsh and Durham quilting, and her encouragement over the possibility of a wider geographical revival of the industry, have proved stimulating in every way.

Many thanks are also due to Miss E. Vigars, of Budleigh Salterton Women's Institute, for the keen interest she has shown, especially in making successful enquiries as to the whereabouts and histories of some of the Devon quilts.

Thanks must be expressed to the owners of quilts for their friendly co-operation and for generously allowing their possessions to be photographed.

The invaluable help of Miss Stamp, for fifty years postmistress at Luppitt, Devon, is gratefully acknowledged; for without her recollections of the local theory, and her personal instruction in the practice of quilting, it would have been difficult to write with confidence from the point of view of a quilter.

Photographs of the three earliest discoveries (Illus. 1, 11, 33, 34, 37, 38), were taken at the request and expense of the Rural Industries Bureau, whose permission to reproduce them is acknowledged with thanks.

Finally, tribute must be paid to the enthusiastic collaboration of my husband, G. D. Gordon Hake, throughout the preparation of this volume. His knowledge of Design, and expert help in measuring and drawing patterns from old quilting, particularly where photography was not possible, have been the means whereby a quantity of somewhat confused material could be co-ordinated and unified in, we hope, a coherent and practical manner.

ELIZABETH HAKE.

Yarcombe, Devon.
December, 1936.

# CONTENTS

# ENGLISH QUILTING
## OLD & NEW

# ENGLISH QUILTING
## OLD & NEW

### CHAPTER I—QUILTING IN THE PAST

THERE seems to be no doubt that quilting is of ancient origin, arising from the daily needs of the peasant class, and developing in more elaborate forms for prosperous members of the community as fashion dictated.

The history of English quilting has been shortly dealt with by several writers. A pamphlet was issued in 1932 by the Victoria and Albert Museum in which the author states that the "word [quilt] can be traced as far back as the thirteenth century at least, and so the making of quilts is undoubtedly an old traditional craft in the British Isles. . . In medieval and later inventories quilts are very often mentioned."[1] Another authority on the history of needlework says that "in May 1540 Katherine Howard, afterwards wife of Henry VIII, received twenty-three quilts of quilted sarsenet out of the Royal Wardrobe, as a sign of Royal favour."[2]

Simultaneously the craft was carried on in most European countries, more especially in Sicily; and in Oriental countries, particularly India, Persia, and in North, East, and West Africa. Referring to foreign influence on English quilting in the seventeenth century the author of *English Secular Embroidery* writes: "In a proclamation of Charles I, in 1631, which enumerated the goods which might be imported from or exported to the East Indies, among the permitted imports are quilts of China, embroidered with gold, quilts of Pitania embroidered with silk, while 'fine Indian quilting and embroidery of silk' at Windsor Castle are mentioned by Celia Fiennes in the reign of William and Mary. . . . Terry in his 'Voyage to the East Indies,' 1655, writes of the people of India: 'The natives there shew very much ingenuity in their curious manufactures. . . . As also in making excellent quilts of their stained cloth, or of fresh coloured taffata lined with their pintadoes (prints or chintz), or of their sattin lined with taffata betwixt which they put cotton wool, and work them together with silk.' "[2]

The history of home quilting in America has been fully examined and recorded in two notably interesting books, *Quilts, their Story and how to make them,* by M. D. Webster (now out of print), and *Old Patchwork Quilts and the Women who make them,* by R. Finley. In these books the

---

[1] *Notes on Quilting,* Victoria and Albert Museum. 1/-.
[2] *English Secular Embroidery,* by M. Jourdain.

writers describe at length the traditional industry brought and carried on by British settlers.

It is possible, as one result of research, tentatively to divide English quilting into three classes, that of the manor (12-15), which often includes very elaborate corded quilting (40-43), the farm (16, 19, 20), and the cottage (39). In the seventeenth and eighteenth centuries the industry seems to have reached its height in technique and popularity, subsiding in the nineteenth century once more into practical means of economy on the part of the humbler housewife, the well-to-do becoming the patrons of the new mechanically-woven fashionable materials.

It has not been easy to get exact information as to the age of most of the examples of quilting illustrated in this book. Only three of the original owner-workers are alive to-day and able to recount the history of their possessions; the others died without bequeathing any written records with their handiwork. The memories of the present owners, reinforced by all the evidence they could collect from friends and relations as to family history, have had to be relied upon for most of the data. For instance, the approximate age of the quilt illustrated in Illus. 33 and 34 was only arrived at through the successful efforts of the present owner in searching for the memorial card on which was inscribed the age at death of her grandmother who made the quilt.

The owner of another quilt (Illus. 1 and 11), in her eighty-third year, found some difficulty in dating what had been treasured as an heirloom since it was left to her when she was eleven, by her aunt who made it. That her aunt died on a Sunday evening was the nearest clue she could provide, until a visit to the aunt's tombstone gave a near indication of the age of the quilt. It was the work of the then village dressmaker, and its patchwork side may therefore be considered an interesting catalogue of contemporary print dress materials.

A quilt made at Colyton, Devon (Illus. 37, 38), has the initials of its worker and date, "A.T., 1825," in minute cross-stitch on the back. Unfortunately not every quilter valued her work enough to take the trouble to incorporate any mark of authorship thereon. On the back of a Herefordshire quilt (Illus. 18), made over a hundred years ago, are the initials of the couple to whom it belonged, and the figure 5, all in cross-stitch, presumably denoting the fifth quilt.

The aged owner of a fine Somerset quilt (copied in Illus. 50), said that she inherited it from her mother-in-law, who made it before her marriage at the age of twenty, in 1820. "She had thirteen children so no time for quilting after she married!"

In an inventory of household belongings, dated 1783, found in an old house in Crewkerne, Somerset, three quilts are mentioned and "a cot quilt and basket."

A very beautiful example of Dorset quilting (Illus. 19, 20), is still in daily use by the elderly grandson of the woman who made it, and he declares that it was shown at an exhibition in London in or about the year 1860, and moreover that it received a third prize. He has no documentary confirmation of this fact, and so far all attempts to identify the exhibition have failed, but such an idée fixe seems unlikely to be without foundation.

Another native of Dorset can remember seeing fine old family quilts in bad repair being used in their last stages under mattresses.

A Wiltshire woman vividly remembers quilts made by her grandmother being worn out on the beds of the grandchildren forty years ago, and has painful recollections of the tediousness of washing heavy quilts in her youth, "all so large, as there were not many single beds in those days."

Some can remember seeing elderly women, "fifty years ago or more," busily working at their quilting frames; and in one Devon family of five

2. Pattern from Fragments of a Devon Quilted Skirt. Black Silk. Made in 1868.

sisters it is recalled that if ever one of them chanced to be idle she was bidden by her mother to "get on with the quilt," which, set up in its frame, formed a normal part of the furniture of most living-rooms. One who lived in North Devon can remember that her mother and her mother's friends made the patchwork sides for their quilts, and passed them on to a neighbour to quilt, for which she charged 3/6 each!

Within a few miles lived another woman who earned her living by the industry, and who is said to have kept a room in her house set apart for her work. This room was always empty except for a chair and a gigantic quilting frame (alleged to have been large enough to stretch a full-sized quilt), which stood on its own four legs, instead of resting on chairs or tables as was the usual custom with smaller frames. "Professional" quilting is said to have been also known in some parts of Cornwall, where as much as 10/-, 15/- or £1 would sometimes be paid for an elaborately worked quilt.

Many of the oldest living generation of West Country women seem able to remember either seeing quilts in use when they were young, long since worn and washed away, or have recollections of hearing of by-gone quilted possessions in their family legends. One Devon dressmaker, aged seventy-five, mentions that her mother received with pride and pleasure a gift from an employer of some pieces of an old petticoat quilted in bright yellow:

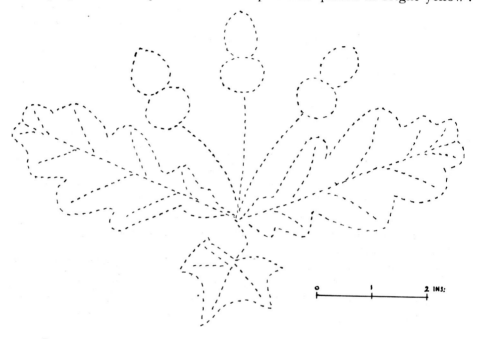

3. PATTERN FROM FRAGMENTS OF A DEVON QUILTED SKIRT. BLACK SILK. MADE IN 1868.

"it must have been thought smart years ago" is her opinion. The same woman possesses fragments of a black silk quilted skirt originally belonging to her aunt (Illus. 2, 3).

A question often asked to-day is how did women have so much time for quilting in the past? Evidence that needlework certainly formed an important part of every woman's equipment from earliest childhood, has reached us through the samplers that are to be found in countless homes to-day, and it is well-known that in large households a quilt designed by the mistress of the house would be worked by her and her daughters and maid-servants, in co-operation. Leisure to many women must have meant time for sewing, and in the country the meagreness of communications with the outside world necessitated relying on occupations and activities that could be carried out at home. The descendant of a family who lived on the Wiltshire Downs says that her great-grandmother used to drive ceremoniously into Marlborough *once a year* only, to shop! It is not surprising that so much patient and contented work could be accomplished with the needle in a world in which noise, speed, and mechanisation were unknown, and women were not expected to express themselves in any but the domestic virtues and fireside crafts.

And presumably life on a farm has always been just as busy as it is now. Judging by family stories and memories it seems that in a great many cases quilts were made by girls between the ages of fifteen and twenty-five, before they married. A girl would begin by being taught by her mother to make what was needed for the family's use, or to repair an old quilt, and by the time she was really proficient she would embark on quilting for her own future home. After her marriage, almost inevitably it appears that no further work of the kind could be undertaken by a young wife until her little daughters grew old enough to learn in their turn from her; and as there was seldom any shortage of daughters the system worked with methodical regularity from generation to generation. Evidence supporting this theory comes from a Somerset quilt owner (16), who says that her grandmother made, with her daughters' help, seven quilts in one winter (1857-8)—one for each daughter! Two of these quilts are said to be now in America.

The very fine corded quilt (43), is known by its possessor to have belonged for several generations to her family, who formerly lived for over three hundred years in Leicestershire, and it is probable that the quilt was made there between a hundred-and-fifty and two hundred years ago.

Quilts can be remembered in a rather remote part of Gloucestershire, and are said to have been of local origin, but so far it has not been possible to obtain any remaining examples.

So much tangible and verbal testimony, though gathered from a somewhat circumscribed area in England, may be considered definitely to point to the likelihood that quilting was a matter of every-day routine in most English homes, great and small, till within the past hundred years.

# CHAPTER II—QUILTING DESIGNS

THE evolution of designs in quilting can only be traced, of course, in imagination. To obtain warmth must undoubtedly have been the original practical purpose of stitching three layers of material together, and the monotony of straight lines forming squares would soon pall for the more enterprising and emotional needlewoman. Even those of limited leisure managed to create works of real artistic value in homely surroundings, and others, with almost unlimited time on their hands no doubt relieved its boredom by elaborating to the utmost extreme their version of the craft, notably in corded quilting, where ornament rather than warmth was the objective to be attained. The two quilts illustrated in Illus. 6 and 46 demonstrate affinity in design and diversity in interpretation; the circumstances of the workers probably differed from each other as widely as it is possible to imagine.

Whereas "hard" quilting, as West Country folk call it (the word "wadded" is used in the North), survived till half way through the nineteenth century, corded quilting appears to have been supplanted at an earlier date by changes in contemporary fashions and fancies on the part of the leisured worker.

One writer, while stating that most women designed their own patterns, says "there were semi-professional designers who would draw them, such as Walter Gale, schoolmaster, of Mayfield, Sussex, who, as his journal shows made money by drawing patterns for quilts, waistcoats, handkerchiefs, etc. :—

'1750. Dec. 26th. I began to draw the quilt belonging to Mrs. Godman.

Dec. 30th. I finished the bed-quilt after five days' close application. It gave satisfaction and I received 10/6 for the drawing.' "

(From the Journal of Walter Gale,
*Sussex Archaeological Collections,* vol. IX.)

A quilt made in New England and finished in 1801 was said to have been designed by a young architect. It would have formed an interesting side-study for the writers on quilting in America to have tabulated, wherever possible, the regional origins of the Settlers who had carried on the traditional designs, perhaps by some such means tracing them to certain counties in England where a local lore in design had been handed from mother to daughter for many generations.

It would rightly be considered rash to generalise on an incompletely explored subject such as British quilting patterns, but it can be said with a measure of confidence that the Welsh traditional designs can usually be identified by their geometrical character (52, 57) those of the North by a freer and more flowing tendency, (53, 58), whereas in Wessex examples hitherto discovered the peculiarity is definitely floral, or naturalistic, notably in the introduction of a central basket of flowers.

In an interesting pamphlet, *The Craft of Quilting in the North Country,* Mrs. Robert Scott writes : "While Northumberland and Durham use so many floral designs, waves, cords and tassels, fans and feathers, the Welsh quilts are noticeable for their geometric patterns, strongly reminiscent of the days of the Vikings." West Country quilting certainly includes many of the details here mentioned as peculiar to the North, but interpreted in characteristically different ways, particularly in their floral motifs. These differences may well be due to climatic influence. In the North the clearly defined, formalised "flowers" are simply and straightforwardly presented with the clear-cut precision and accuracy associated with the people of that hardier climate; whereas the West Country flowing borders and more realistic floral centres are worked in a rather haphazard way suggestive of the easy-going nature of the Southerner. This often shows itself at the corners, always a test for the designer, where the junction of patterns, or change of direction is handled with nonchalance, which, while introducing a spirit of freedom, lacks the carefully planned effect of the Northern examples. In Illus. 38 will be seen the illustration of a quilt whose designer set out to do a good deal that she failed to accomplish (perhaps expressing her temperament), yet not without achieving a general sense of composition.

According to the aged quilters already alluded to on a previous page, floral designs in the West were made from nature. One of them recalls the fact that her mother and grandmother used to pick sprays of oak leaves, ivy, clover, and even thistles, bringing them home to study in the evenings before making the great decision as to which should form the basis of the design for a new quilt. If oak was the final choice it was usual to combine it with ivy—"as they grow together" (2, 3).

Another quilter states that in her designs, sixty years ago, she followed to a great extent the pattern dictated by her patchwork, thus producing a geometrical effect (22, 23). The more general custom, however, appears to have been to ignore the patchwork as pattern, and to treat it as a piece of many-coloured material forming the showy side of the quilt. The days and ways of all the "Easy-to-make," "Best-Way," "Needlecraft" literature and mechanically produced transfers being unknown till within recent years, the country needlewoman naturally found inspiration for her designs in simple familiar surroundings, and moreover, not only felt no difficulty in interpreting them, but in nine cases out of ten she would seem to have been endowed with an innate instinct for formalism and design, which to-day might well be the envy of many whose spontaneity has been killed and whose eyes have been blinded by mass-produced patterns.

An exceptional example of old Welsh quilting, now in Bristol (44, 45), illustrates this point. The quilt was made in a small seaside village in Cardiganshire (hitherto unexplored for quilting history) by the wife of a fisherman. According to legend, he, at the time the quilt was being made, was away at sea for many weeks, leaving his wife with her mind and eyes continually concentrated on the ocean, with the result that she introduced the obvious little wave-rhythm seen in the design of her quilt. No other instance of this particular pattern appears to be known at present.

Sentiment or superstition played its inevitable contemporary part in quilting; hearts (1, 16), were sometimes included in the design of a marriage quilt, and if a cable or spray of foliage (1, 29) formed part of a border, it was desirable that it should be unbroken, the belief being held that a broken cable foretold a life cut short by disaster. "If a girl has not made a quilt before she is twenty-one no man will want to marry her" was an old Devon saying.

After considering these remarks referring to separate patterns and designs, their immediate origins, and symbolism associated with them, those workers who have studied the subject of Design will appreciate the fact that the success of a composition depends on the right application of certain principles to which the motifs of the design are subservient.

It might therefore be useful to outline those principles, both as an aid to designing new quilts and appreciating the arrangement of old examples.

Firstly then it must be remembered that the size and shape of the quilt are the determining factors of the design. It is a space to be filled. So that this filling shall be orderly and effective the principle of Subordination must be applied. This involves a dominant idea to which all else is subordinate. If patterns were applied indiscriminately to the surface of a quilt, the result would be chaos : a muddle. The application of the principle of Subordination reduces confusion to order, complexity to unity.

A glance at many of the examples illustrated in this book will show the importance of this orderly lay-out. It will be seen, for instance, that the bold border and dominant central motif stand out by their spacing and size in relation to the rest of the quilt. Contributing to this result also is the use of such other principles as Contrast, both in size and shape, and Symmetry, or Balance, not necessarily involving repetition.

Fully to understand the peculiar difficulties of the would-be quilt designer it is impossible to over-emphasise the importance of these governing principles, and the necessity for bearing in mind the type, function, and limitations of the materials to be used. A good quilt designer knows that the fundamental and practical object of her pattern is to keep three layers of material in position, giving a pleasing effect of design without leaving large unstitched spaces. To achieve this result most careful planning and forethought are needed.

One of the tests of good application of quilt-design, as has already been said in this chapter, is in "turning the corners" of the pattern. The success or failure of this test is specially marked in borders (1, 9).

The problem of covering a large piece of material with close stitching without blurring the main theme of the design, provides another pitfall for the inexperienced quilter. This difficulty can often be overcome by means of a double line of sewing round the essential motifs of the pattern, and further emphasising their importance by filling the background with a geometrical design on a smaller scale, based on curves or their intersections, such as the "shell" and "wineglass" (8), or intersecting straight lines forming squares or diamonds. The choice of such "filling" should be made with a view to contrast, squares and diamonds serving as a foil to a curved design, and the "shell" and "wineglass" setting off a rectangular motif. These four "filling" or background designs are not peculiar to any one region in England, but occur wherever traditional quilting is to be found.

There should be an almost boundless field open to the quilt designer in evolving new motifs and patterns, or in adapting old designs, but their application and proportion should be governed by the principles suggested in this chapter.

SCALE OF ⌞⌟⌞⌟⌞⌟⌞⌟ INCHES

4. Centre of a Wiltshire Quilt in White Silk. 18th Century.

If a regional survey of English quilting could be accomplished doubtless much scope would be found for the interchange of local idiom in patterns. The contribution of the West of England to this pooling of designs would be of great value, because its hereditary custom of designing from nature would provide an inexhaustible supply of new ideas and subjects from which to draw for patterns. The West in its turn might profitably absorb more of the sculptural and severely formalised qualities of the Northern designs, and some of the intricate geometrical patterns expressed in Welsh quilting. It is not unlikely that hitherto unknown traditional designs might be discovered in unexplored counties.

# CHAPTER III—QUILT MAKING

"Old woman, old woman, are you fond of carding?"
(From *The Deaf Woman's Courtship*, traditional song.)

THE first essential of a quilter's equipment is a frame, for without one even small objects such as tea-cosies and cushions are liable to pull out of shape. Modern quilters seem unanimously to consider an ordinary embroidery frame satisfactory for this type of work and sometimes, for purposes of economy, an unwanted picture-frame can be adapted.

The drawing (5) shows the traditional frame most commonly used in the past in Devon, Somerset and Cornwall, and closely resembles that still used to-day in the Northern districts. An interesting exception may be mentioned from the reminiscences of a North Devon farmer's wife, who as a child used to watch a neighbour working on a much larger frame, containing a quilt about 7ft. 6ins. square, stretched to its full size. This frame stood on its own four legs, and almost filled the room in which it was kept. The drawing (6) represents the centre of a quilt made on this frame about seventy years ago.

The frame, which seems to have been the standardised one of its day, circa 1800 (5), consists of two deal bars, each having a strip of webbing nailed to one of its edges. Two "swords," as they were locally called, made of oak or other hardwood, each perforated by a series of equally spaced holes, are slipped through slots at each end of both bars. These equally spaced holes enable any given distance between the bars to be established by the simple means of inserting four hard-wood pegs, two in each sword at the inside corners of the bars. Thus the quilting-frame becomes rigid and parallel-sided. Such a frame as this can be made, as it always was, by any village carpenter for a few shillings. The size of frame shown in the diagram can be modified according to individual needs.

Having acquired a frame the wool for interlining must be prepared. Some form of wadding or mechanically prepared cotton wool was sometimes used in part of North Devon and in certain Cornish districts, as it is to-day in the North of England, but home grown lambswool, and often an old blanket, were the general rule, the former by the finer needlewomen; and elderly women say they can remember being sent in their young days to collect lambswool from the hedges, because it was always considered by expert quilters to be the softest for sewing. According to one Cornish account wadding would be used in addition to a blanket, if the latter was very thin and worn "so that would raise the flowers or design, when stitched." From this same source it is declared that lambswool was too expensive locally to use forty years ago. In Wales to-day lambswool is still invariably used.

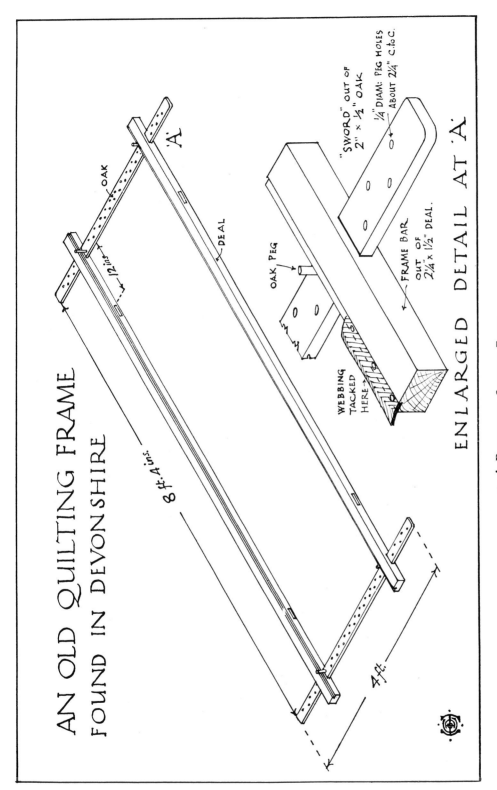

AN OLD QUILTING FRAME
FOUND IN DEVONSHIRE

8 ft. 4 ins.

4 ft.

12 ins.

OAK

DEAL

'A'

OAK PEG

WEBBING
TACKED
HERE

"SWORD" OUT OF
2" × ½" OAK

¼" DIAM: PEG HOLES
ABOUT 2¼" c.to.C.

FRAME BAR
OUT OF
2¼" × 1½" DEAL.

ENLARGED DETAIL AT 'A'

5. A DEVONSHIRE QUILTING FRAME.

About 2 lbs. of wool would fill a large quilt, less than 1½ lbs. should be enough for a single bed size. It must be thoroughly scoured in soapy water, and after several rinsings, dried out of doors on a sunny breezy day, usually spread on the ground under a wire- or fish-net covering to prevent it from blowing away. When dry it should still contain a proportion of its natural oil, which, tradition claims, safeguards it from the ravages of moth.

SCALE OF |+++|+++|+++|+++| INCHES

6. Centre of a Devon Quilt in White Linen. Circa 1866.
Note the bold Version of the Shell Pattern.

Teasing or carding the wool is the next process, and a lengthy one. A pair of wire brushes (49), are more efficient and speedy than pulling by hand. (The quilter whose work is seen in Illus. 22, 23, says she always teased her wool by hand.) All knots and lumps should be brushed out carefully, and the wool finally picked over by hand to ensure perfect cleanliness. Those who do not feel inclined to tackle the preparation of their own wool can of course buy it ready scoured and carded.

The materials for the top and back of a quilt should be chosen with careful judgment, and should both be of the same weight and texture, whether in silk or cotton. Artificial and very shiny silks, in the experience of present day quilters, are to be avoided, as they do not turn out well. Good Shanghai and Tyrian silks can be recommended; also some "vat-dyed" and "wild" silks which wash and wear well. Really good qualities of crêpe de chine and dull satin can be used, but are expensive. For very simple tastes the best casement cloths are suitable, and for those who prefer something rather "shinier" than casement, yet less costly than silk, there is a satisfactory form of poplin in mercerised cotton, which can be obtained at a very reasonable price, and is much used to-day for quilts, though it is considered too heavy for smaller work such as dressing-gowns or cushions. Sateen, which seems popular with Northern quilters, is effective, but the work should justify the best materials.

The West Country tradition for backing materials varied, but plain white linen predominated. In Cornwall it is reported that "the old Paisley material was a very favourite thing for the back of patched quilts, and quilting wouldn't spoil the pattern of the material."

When chosen the material for the back of the quilt should be tacked at each end to the webbing on both bars of the frame, and one end rolled round its bar until the material is stretched taut from bar to bar, which distance is controlled by the pegs in the swords. Tape must be pinned to the remaining edges of the material and laced round the swords (48).

The third layer of material, the top, is traditionally often coloured in contrast to a white back, and in the past was frequently composed of elaborate patchwork, or sometimes of large remnants of old hand-embroidered materials contrived into the exact dimensions required for the quilt. By these means the contents of the household piece-bag were converted into a thrifty substitute for new material. A custom prevailed in one Cornish district of buying remnants of prints at a cost of 1/4 per lb.

It may sometimes be wise to add to the substance of a thin silk material by tacking it to a lining of butter-muslin, which serves as interlining between the silk and lambswool. This practice was apparently often adopted in quilted skirts, which can still be remembered by many of the oldest generation to-day. One guinea was the standard fee charged for quilting a skirt, in a village near Honiton seventy years ago.

The study of patchwork would form a fascinatingly digressive subject covering a wide field, for which there is not space in this volume. The West Country regional characteristics do not betray any exciting surprises, and the examples so far discovered, with two notable exceptions in Illus. 26, 28, consist mainly of squares, triangles, "boxes" and "logs." Hexa-gons (varyingly described by aged quilt owners as "optigons," "octicians," and "sextains"), appear in some instances in the centre of a patchwork quilt, but towards the outer borders the enthusiasm and energy of the design seem to trail off into larger piecing of odd squares and strips.

A delightful summary of the peculiar interest and charm of patchwork from a needleworker's point of view, is given by M. D. Webster in her

*Quilts, their Story and how to make them,* when she quotes from Eliza Calvert Hall's *Aunt Jane of Kentucky:* "How much piecin' a quilt is like livin' a life! Many a time I've set and listened to Parson Page preachin' about predestination and free will, and I've said to myself, 'If I could jest git up in the pulpit with one of my quilts I could make it a heap plainer to folks than parson's makin' it with his big words.' You see, you start out with jest so much caliker; you don't go to the store and pick it out and buy it, but the neighbours will give you a piece here and a piece there, and you'll have a piece left over every time you cut a dress, and you take jest what happens to come. And that's like predestination. But when it comes to the cuttin' out, why, you're free to choose your own pattern. You can give the same kind of pieces to two persons, and one'll make a 'nine-patch' and one'll make a 'wild-goose-chase,' and there'll be two quilts made out of the same kind of pieces, and jest as different as they can be. And that's jest the way with livin'. The Lord sends us the pieces, but we can cut them out and put them together pretty much to suit ourselves, and there's a heap more in the cuttin' out and the sewin' than there is in the caliker."

The top material, whether plain, patterned, or patch-work must next be tacked or pinned to the webbing at one end only, leaving the other end free, while the wool is spread evenly on to the inner side of the stretched back material.

At this point it is of great importance to make a written note of the exact dimensions of the quilt-to-be, allowing for a good turn-in of all its raw edges corresponding to the amount of edge tacked on to the webbing. To be able to refer to these measurements as the design proceeds is the only method whereby to ensure equal spacing for repetition and symmetry without unrolling the already quilted portion of the work.

The top material must in its turn be stretched over the wool as tightly as possible, and pinned towards the opposite bar, the remaining loose end being rolled back and pinned to keep it in position until it has gradually to be unrolled as the quilting progresses from the tacked end to the loose end.

To be used comfortably with a minimum of fatigue and muscular strain, the frame must be placed at a congenial height to the worker. In the photograph (48) it will be noticed that one bar is resting on a table, and the other, the end that is being worked, balances on the arms of the quilter's chair.

All quilting seems to have been, and still is, worked from the right side or top material, never from the back.

The quilting design having been decided upon, templates of its various motifs and units must be cut out in stiff cardboard (see Illus. 10) and the two traditional ways of using these templates are optional. The older tradition is to place the template on the top material and scratch closely round its outline with a needle. When the template is removed the scratched line should show clearly enough to be sewn through. A later custom, very prevalent in the West, especially when the top layer of material was coloured, was to rub chalk round all the edges of the template, which, when pressed on to the material, left in chalk the outline marked for sewing. Tailor's chalk is very generally used to-day, and is much more clearly seen, especially on silk, than the scratch-line of a needle.

Rather than sewing silk, No. 40 cottons should be used for *all* materials. No one would notice that the stitches are in cotton, which has been proved to be in every way more satisfactory for working than silk. Specially short needles are necessary, not more than $1\frac{1}{8}$ inches long. These are easily obtainable and are often known as "between needles." Knots in the cotton should only be made when near the raw edges where they can be hidden. Otherwise throughout the work the ends of cotton, after a back-stitch has been made, should be left nearly 2 inches out of the material, both in beginning and in ending-off, and be coaxed with a needle through the top material into the wool.

Opinions appear to differ as to where the sewing should actually begin, but a majority are convinced that corners provide the best starting point, working either from foot to head or from side to side of the quilt. In one North Devon instance it is averred that the worker (whose handiwork is illustrated in Illus. 6) began in the centre of her quilts, working thence outwards to the edges. This method also obtained in some parts of Cornwall, in order, it is stated, to avoid "puckering." In the traditional quilting districts to-day working from one side to the other seems generally favoured.

In the past, where the habit of using chalk prevailed, the whole design was, in rare cases, marked out before the sewing began, but usually, as it is to-day, the pattern would be marked in portions not more than 10 to 12 inches deep from the end at which the sewing started, the marking continuing as the quilt proceeded, and the chalk lines being brushed off as the sewing was accomplished. For marking squares or diamonds in the old method a piece of fine string rubbed in chalk was extended from a pin at each end, and when "snapped" up and down like a violin string, would leave its mark in chalk clearly enough to be followed in sewing. To-day a long ruler is commonly used.

The exact form of stitchery is aptly described in Mrs. Robert Scott's pamphlet, already quoted, as "a running or darning stitch, not a stab stitch." Two or three stitches at a time can be run, and the first finger of the left hand must be held under the frame to be pricked each time the needle pierces the three layers of material, in this way securing them together with such perfect regularity of stitching as to make it impossible to say from which side the quilting was sewn. This sacrifice of left hand fingers sounds more painful than it is in reality, as a hardening process soon takes place, and after a short time, except in rather rare instances, very little of the pricking is felt. Evenness in spacing the stitches is a criterion of good quilting and can only be acquired gradually, after a considerable amount of patient practice. Neither can speed be easily achieved by the inexperienced quilter, but should increase with familiarity and improving skill. The alternatives to the running stitch are back stitch and chain stitch, but these are unsightly on the wrong side, and therefore should be used only for objects which are not required to be reversible, as in the past they were sometimes used in quilted petticoats.

It will be found that it is only possible to sew to a depth of about 11 inches at a time from the edge of the frame. When this section has been quilted it must be rolled over its bar, and the same amount of unquilted materials unrolled and stretched at the other end. A movable piece of muslin is useful and traditional to place on the finished work as it is rolled over, to protect it from being rubbed by the sleeve of the worker.

When the quilt has been completed and taken off the frame, the raw edges of both top and back should be neatly turned in and tacked, then sewn together by two rows of running stitch about $\frac{1}{8}$ inch apart, as shown in the diagram (7).

The methods described in these pages apply to all wadded quilting, whether for bed-quilts, dressing-jackets, cushions or other objects. For garments and tea-cosies the quilting should be worked on the material before it is cut into the exact portions required, so as to leave a margin for seams.

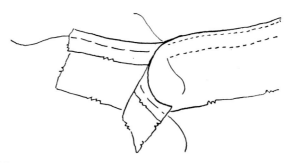

7. TRADITIONAL RUNNING STITCH METHOD OF FINISHING RAW EDGES.

Cutting out before the quilting was done, then stretching on a frame to quilt, would inevitably pull the material out of shape.

A word must be said about corded quilting, often called Italian quilting. Whether it originated in Italy or elsewhere, the fact that it was as prevalent in England as in any other European country during the seventeenth and eighteenth centuries seems incontestible. Yet in spite of the existence of many very beautiful examples of this work in museums and private hands in this country, it is difficult to obtain inherited information as to its technique.

The materials consisted, as they do in the revival to-day, of two layers of material, usually fine white linen, sewn together by an intricate and elaborate design—often arabesque—worked by means of two rows of backstitching about $\frac{1}{4}$ inch apart, forming a narrow duct into which the cord was pushed through small holes cut at intervals in the back material. This work is therefore not reversible. The illustration (43) gives some idea of the effect on the right side of the work when the inserted cord stands out in relief. The minute and accurate stitchery, comparable with that of the present day sewing machine, must have entailed countless months of work on one object, and encourages the belief that this type of quilting was the prerogative of women who had a considerable amount of leisure at their disposal. The lack of warmth in corded quilting also supports the obvious theory that ornament was its authors' chief aim, and they achieved it by exquisitely patient craftsmanship and delicate taste in design (40-42).

Wherever possible those wishing to learn quilting to-day would do well to have a few lessons from an experienced quilter rather than to rely entirely on written directions.

# CHAPTER IV
## QUILTING TO-DAY AND TO-MORROW

ALL hand needlework, from having formed an integral part of normal routine in every English household, has dwindled into a pastime for those who have leisure to pursue it, and that it should resume its former status is neither to be expected nor desired, as the essence of its merit is that it is *hand* work, and therefore unsuited for competition with work that is better performed by machinery. That as a *hobby* needlework of every kind is increasing to-day is noticeable in the growing number of exhibitors whose work is to be seen at most contemporary exhibitions of any importance. In this connection quilting has lately received much attention, and the fascination of this type of work experienced by those who have mastered its technique, encourages the hope that the revival is genuine and likely to be lasting. The standard attained in quilting at its best to-day is as high as ever in its history. This claim is borne out by the very lovely examples of quilts, cushions, and so forth to be seen in the photographs reproduced in Illus. 50, 51, etc.

Wadded quilting has essentially more practical qualities than corded or linen quilting, and is certainly the more popular of the two to-day, but the very fine examples of the latter shown at recent exhibitions of modern needlework, contribute worthily to the history of this type of work, which, it is to be hoped, may continue to thrive.

There are, moreover, indications that leisure, which for so long has been the privilege of the few, is to be extended by legislation to within the grasp of many women and girls employed in industrial centres, and it is not unlikely to be accompanied by a desire to devote some of it to the practice of creative forms of handiwork.

In the distressed areas of Wales and the North of England many homes have been kept intact by the gallant efforts of the very skilful quilting members of families whose normal breadwinners have suffered several recent years of unemployment, and although it is difficult to foresee how general a revival of English quilting, as a home craft, may become, there are signs of awakening interest in many parts of the country.

In rural districts, where tradition lingers, and where mechanised pleasures are still rare, and not always uncritically appreciated, there is a distinct movement towards attempting to revive what appeals to most women as one of the thrifty and enduring home industries.

Through the comprehensive machinery of Women's Institutes in most villages in the British Isles, and the less mature but growing number of Townswomen's Guilds, quilting, in the Welsh and Northern traditions, is being taught and learned with diligence, and with outstandingly successful results, by women of varying degrees of leisure, and every shade of competence and taste, who realise that through them this fine national heritage can be carried on and developed.

It is impossible to emphasise too strongly the desirability of this development being continued on traditional lines.   Rightfully there should be no short-cut methods in this particular branch of needlework.   The worker should plan her own designs, with templates, as described in chapters II and III, and not have recourse to untraditional ready-made patterns stamped by transfers on muslin; one disadvantage of these being that the muslin forms the back layer of material and has to be covered with a lining : the quilting therefore only shows on one side of the finished work.

Quilting by outlining the design of a patterned chintz or cretonne, sometimes seen to-day, can hardly be regarded as a legitimate descendant of the parent craft, and may be considered but a makeshift substitute for the traditional method.

As in the past so to-day, quilting inherently provides infinite scope for truly creative pleasure in design and execution.

The owner of the frame shown (5) says that it would have been destroyed, or might have perished from lack of use, left to rot in a wood-shed, had not her mother, on her deathbed, asked to have it brought to her in order that she might once more see the frame on which she had produced work that had given her as much pleasure as anything she had experienced in the course of her earthly activities.

"In its suitability for manufacture within the home, the quilt possesses a peculiar merit.   Although exposed for a full century to the competition of machinery, under the depressing influence of which most of the fireside crafts have all but vanished, the making of quilts as a home industry [in America] has never languished. . . . As a home-maker, the quilt is a most capable tool lying ready at the hand of every woman.   The selection of design, the care in piecing, the patience in quilting; all make for feminine contentment and domestic happiness."[1]

[1] *Quilts: Their Story and how to Make Them*, M. D. Webster.

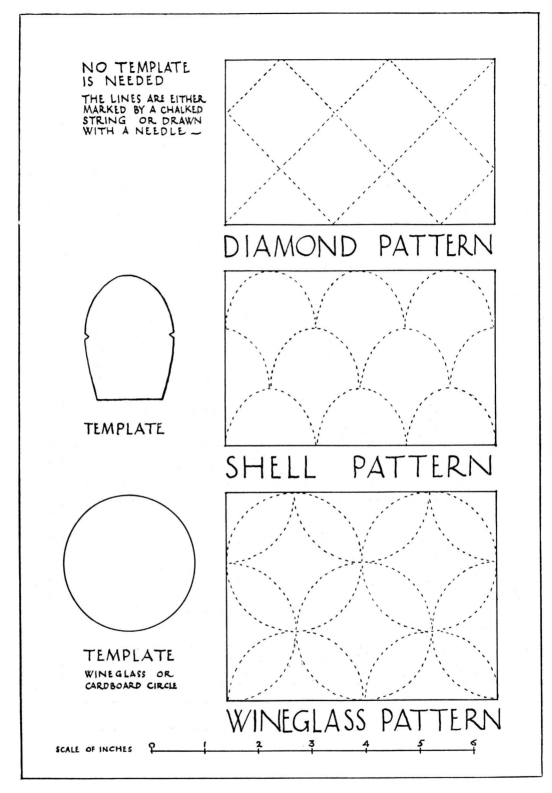

NO TEMPLATE
IS NEEDED

THE LINES ARE EITHER
MARKED BY A CHALKED
STRING OR DRAWN
WITH A NEEDLE —

DIAMOND PATTERN

TEMPLATE

SHELL PATTERN

TEMPLATE
WINEGLASS OR
CARDBOARD CIRCLE

WINEGLASS PATTERN

SCALE OF INCHES   0   1   2   3   4   5   6

8. THREE EXAMPLES OF TRADITIONAL "FILLING" OR BACKGROUND DESIGNS.

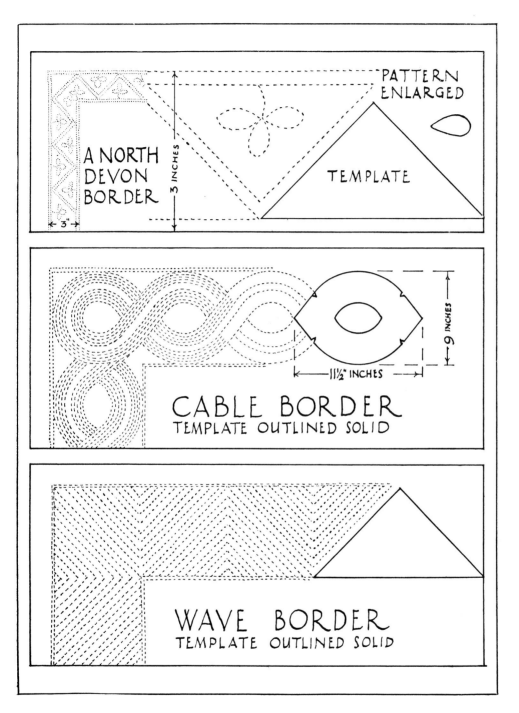

PATTERN ENLARGED

A NORTH DEVON BORDER

3 INCHES

TEMPLATE

3"

CABLE BORDER
TEMPLATE OUTLINED SOLID

9 INCHES

11½" INCHES

WAVE BORDER
TEMPLATE OUTLINED SOLID

9. THREE TRADITIONAL BORDER PATTERNS.

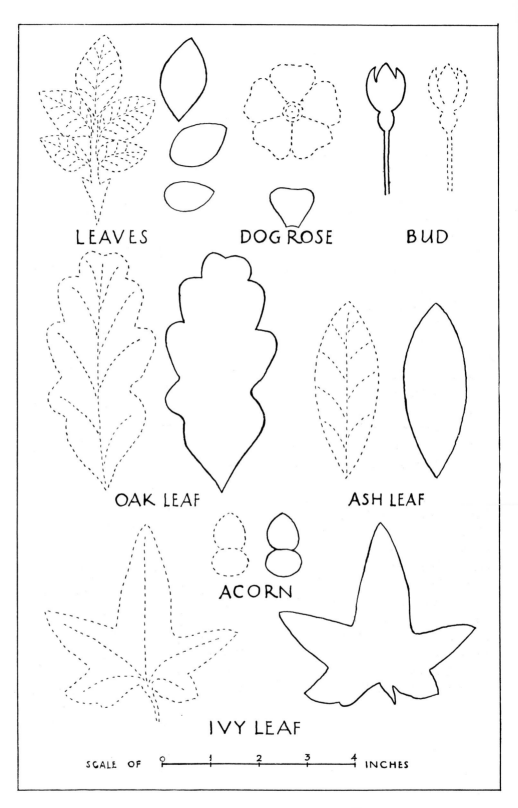

LEAVES    DOG ROSE    BUD

OAK LEAF    ASH LEAF

ACORN

IVY LEAF

SCALE OF  0  1  2  3  4  INCHES

10. SOME CHARACTERISTIC FLORAL MOTIFS AND THEIR TEMPLATES.

# INDEX

*The numerals in italic denote the figure numbers of the illustrations.*

11. Devon Quilt, circa 1840. Patchwork made from Dressmaker's Piece-bag.
(*See Frontispiece.*)

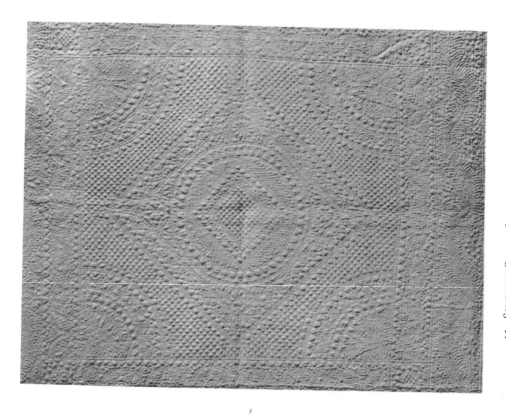

13. Somerset Quilt, 1807. White Linen both sides.

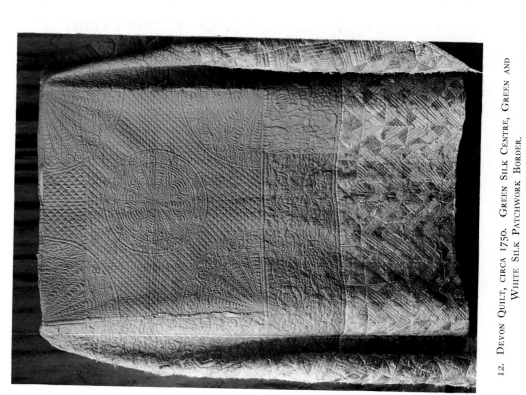

12. Devon Quilt, circa 1750. Green Silk Centre, Green and
White Silk Patchwork Border.

Examples of Fan Corners and Geometrical Centres.

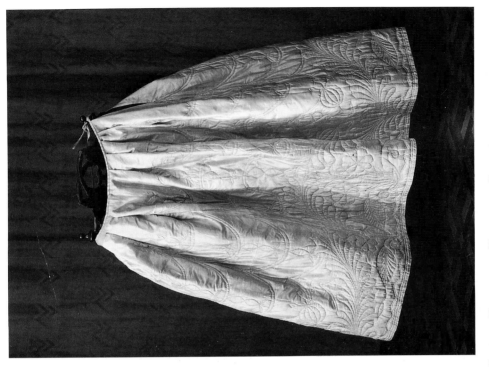

14, 15. A Silk Quilted Petticoat, Devon, circa 1780. Note the Naturalistic Tendency in Design.

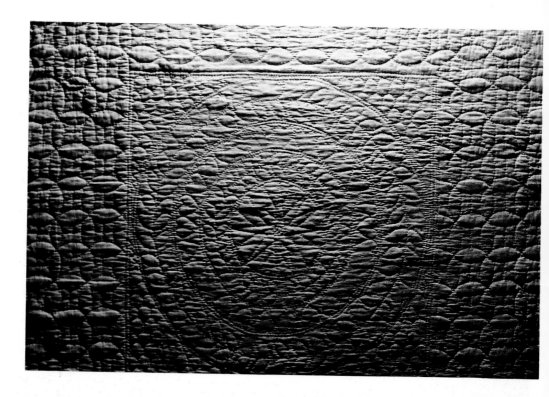

16, 17. PART OF A SOMERSET QUILT, 1857, IN PATCHWORK BACKED WITH WHITE LINEN; ONE OF
SEVEN MADE BY ONE FAMILY DURING A SINGLE WINTER. NOTE THE QUILTED CIRCLE OF HEARTS
BETWEEN TWO CIRCLES OF LEAVES.

18. Herefordshire Quilt, Early 19th Century. Bands of Mauve Chintz and White Linen.

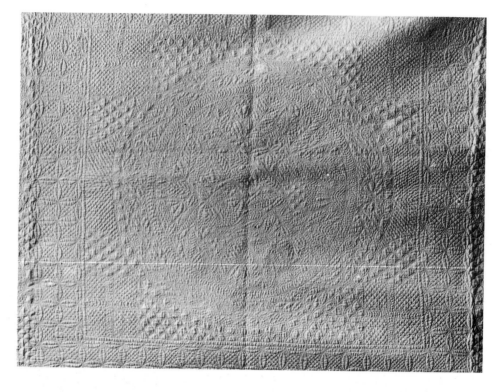

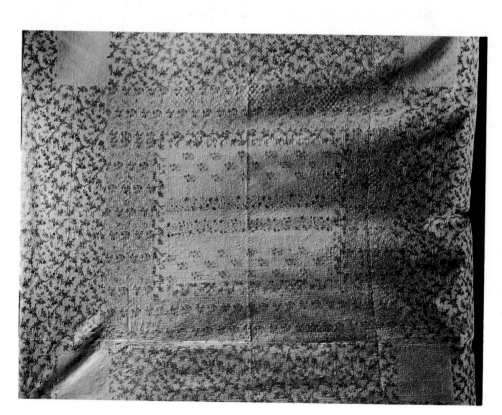

19, 20. Dorset Quilt, circa 1815. Patchwork side in large pieces of Chintz, White Linen Back, Floral Centre.

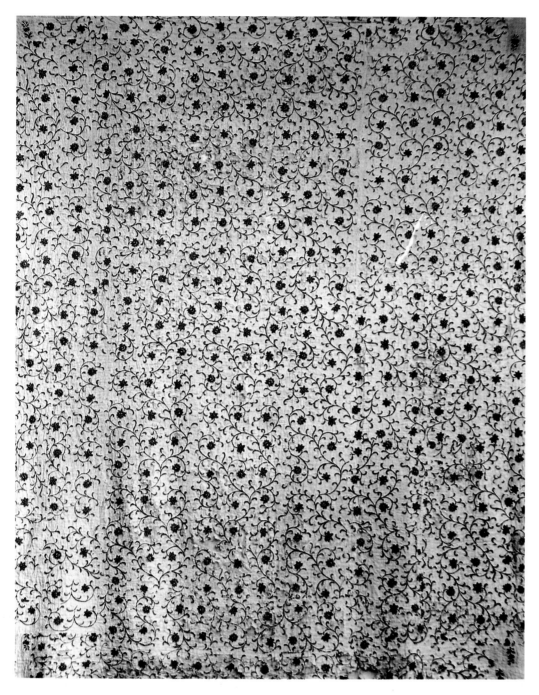

21. "PATCHWORK" SIDE OF A DEVON QUILT, 18TH CENTURY. AN EXAMPLE OF THE USE OF REMNANTS OF OLD EMBROIDERY INSTEAD OF ODD PIECES. IN THIS CASE THE EMBROIDERY, IN EXQUISITE RED AND BLUE SILK ON LINEN, IS CONSIDERABLY OLDER THAN THE QUILT.

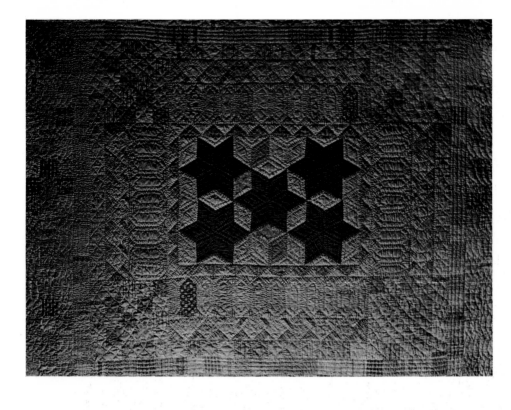

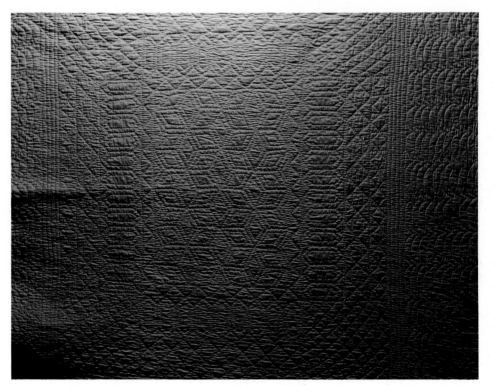

22, 23. SOMERSET QUILT, CIRCA 1875. PATCHWORK IN CHINTZ AND TURKEY RED, WHITE LINEN BACK. QUILTING PATTERN FOLLOWS THE PATCHWORK.

25. HEREFORDSHIRE QUILT, EARLY 19TH CENTURY. PATCHWORK IN COLOURED PRINTS.

24. CORNISH QUILT, 1837. PATCHWORK IN COLOURED SILKS.

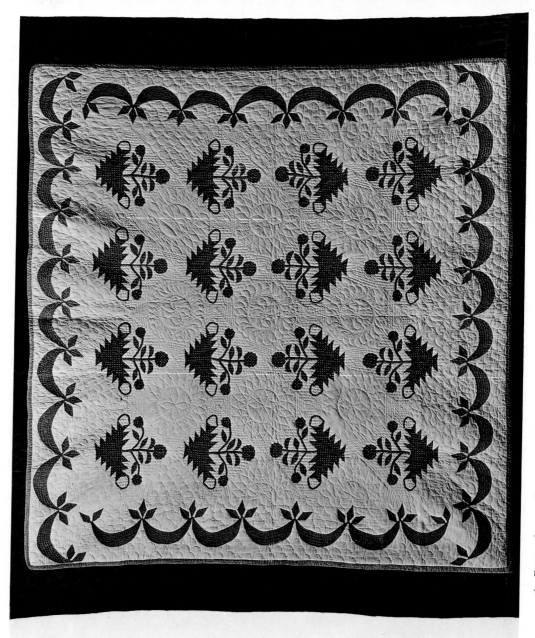

26. Devon Quilt. Early 19th Century. Appliqué Patchwork in Red and Green Prints on White Linen.

27.  DEVON QUILT.  WHITE LINEN BACK OF QUILT SHOWN IN ILLUS. 26.

28. SOMERSET QUILT, CIRCA 1850. PATCHWORK SIDE IN TURKEY RED AND WHITE, "PETER AND PAUL" PATTERN.

29. SOMERSET QUILT. BORDER OF "WAVE" AND CLOVER LEAF.

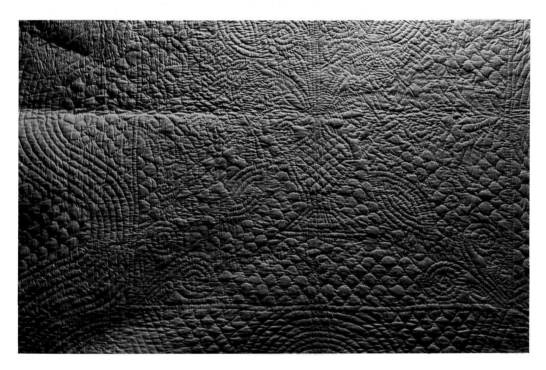

30. SOMERSET QUILT. FLORAL CENTRE.

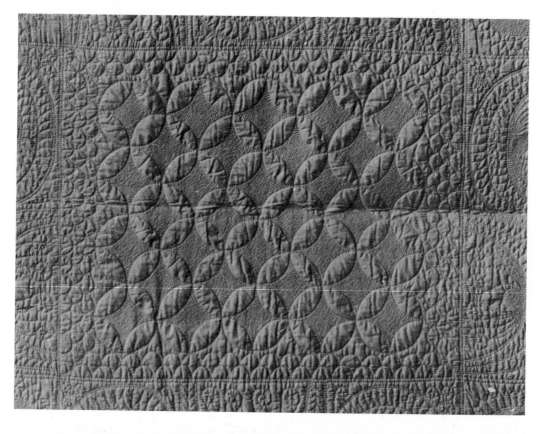

31, 32. Devon Quilt in White Linen, Late 19th Century. Made in Three Weeks. Corners showing angles of Borders, Centre showing Wine Glass Pattern. Note close Stitching used as Contrast.

33, 34. Devon Quilt, circa 1875. Patchwork backed with White Linen, Quilted in Geometrical Patterns, somewhat Welsh in Character.

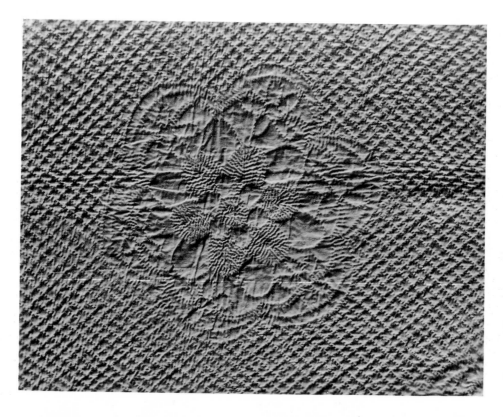

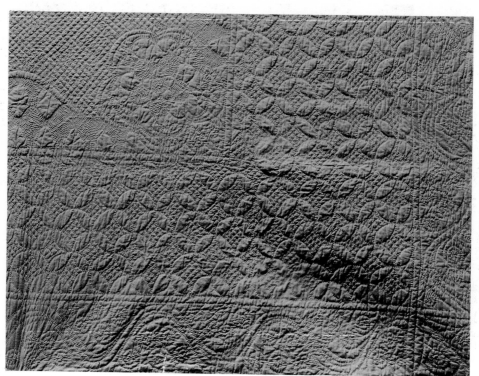

35, 36. Devon Quilt, 1810. Centre with Diamond Pattern "Filling" and part of Border.

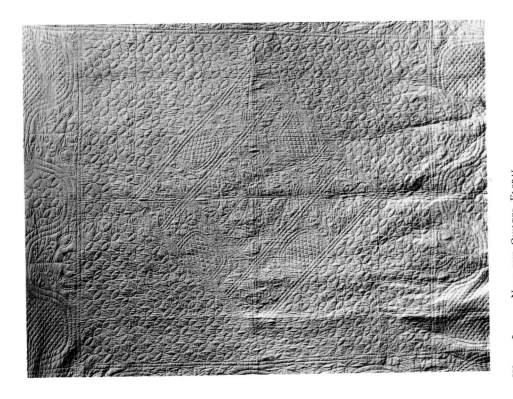

37, 38. Devon Qult, 1825. In Patchwork and White Linen. Note the Quilted Floral Centre and "Wine Glass" Filling.

39. DEVON QUILT, CIRCA 1850. AN EXAMPLE OF WEST COUNTRY TEMPERAMENT IN DESIGN. TYPICAL FLORAL CENTRE.

40. PORTION OF WILTSHIRE CORDED QUILT, EARLY 18TH CENTURY. WHITE LINEN. PHOTOGRAPHED AS A TRANSPARENCY.

41. FRAGMENT OF WILTSHIRE QUILTING. TWO PIECES OF LINEN QUILTED IN BACKSTITCH. NO CORD INSERTED, 18TH CENTURY. PHOTOGRAPHED AS A TRANSPARENCY.

42. English Corded Quilt, Early 18th Century. White Linen. Photographed as a
Transparency.

43. CENTRE OF A LEICESTERSHIRE CORDED QUILT, 18TH CENTURY. WHITE LINEN.

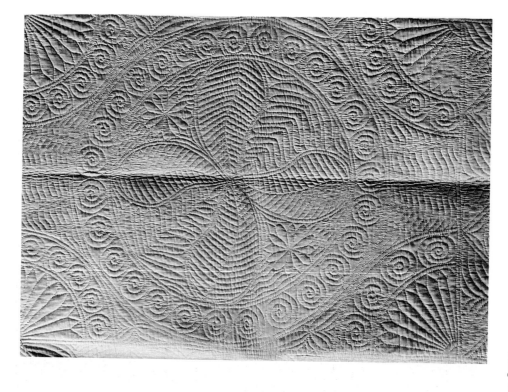

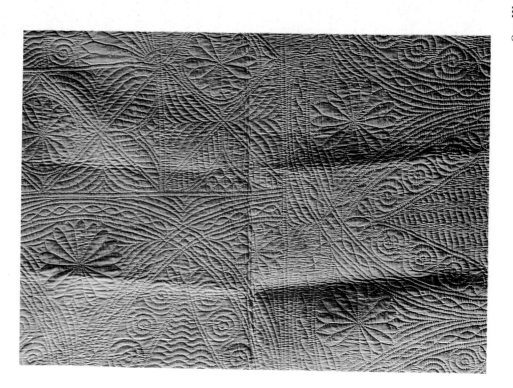

OLD WELSH QUILT.

44. PORTION OF BORDER SHOWING "CHURCH WINDOW" MOTIF. 45. GEOMETRICAL CENTRE WITH "SEA-WAVE" FILLING.

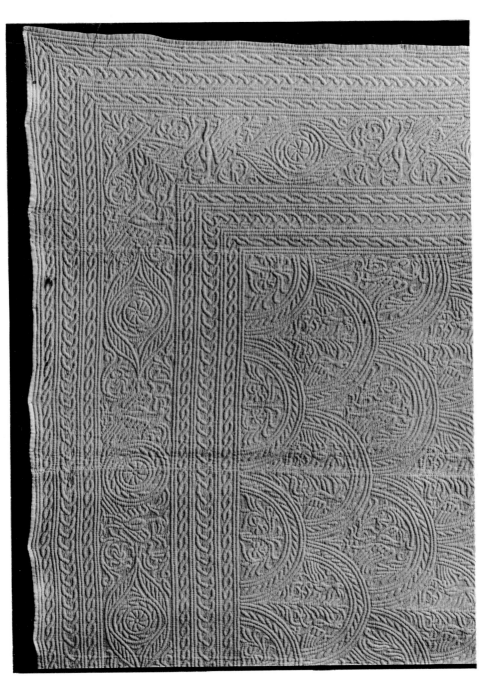

46. PART OF PORTUGUESE COVERLET. CORDED QUILTING, 17TH CENTURY.
[*By courtesy of the Victoria and Albert Museum.*

47. Indian Quilt made by Himalayan Women, circa 1922. White Linen, Backstitched, Interlined with Semal Cotton. Note the Relationship to English Quilting Patterns.

48. THE QUILTER AT WORK. BIRD'S EYE VIEW SHOWING QUILTING FRAME SET UP AND THE WORKER IN POSITION.

49. CARDING THE WOOL.

50. Copy by the Porth Group of Welsh Quilters (1935) of a Somerset Quilt made in 1818.
Note Floral Design and Centre.

51. NORTHUMBRIAN QUILTED CUSHIONS.

[*By courtesy of the Dryad Press.*

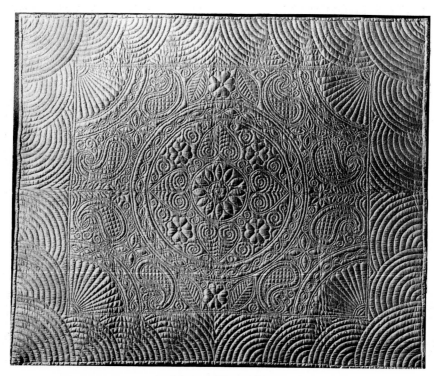

52. MODERN WELSH QUILT.

[*By courtesy of the Dryad Press.*

53. MODERN NORTHUMBRIAN QUILT.

[*By courtesy of the Dryad Press.*

54. CUSHION, DURHAM.

55. COT QUILT, S. WALES.

56. DRESSING JACKET, NORTHUMBERLAND. IN SHANGHAI SILK.

[*By courtesy of the Rural Industries Bureau.*

58. A Durham Feather Pattern. The Feathers used in the Centre are perhaps the best known North Country Pattern. Feather-wreath in Border.

[*By courtesy of The Rural Industries Bureau.*]

57. A Typical Welsh Pattern. By Porth Group, Rhondda Valley.

[*By courtesy of The Rural Industries Bureau.*]